Juan Ramón Jiménez

by HOWARD T. YOUNG

 *Columbia University Press*
NEW YORK & LONDON 1967

COLUMBIA ESSAYS ON MODERN WRITERS is a series of critical studies of English, Continental, and other writers whose works are of contemporary artistic and intellectual significance.

Editor: William York Tindall

Advisory Editors

Jacques Barzun   W. T. H. Jackson   Joseph A. Mazzeo   Justin O'Brien

Juan Ramón Jiménez is number 28 of the series

HOWARD T. YOUNG is Professor of Romance Languages at Pomona College and author of *The Victorious Expression,* a study of contemporary Spanish poetry.

For Laurie

Copyright © 1967 Columbia University Press
Library of Congress Catalog Card Number: 67-27361
Printed in the United States of America

Grateful acknowledgment is made to Francisco H.-Pinzón Jiménez for permission to quote from the works of Juan Ramón Jiménez, to Harcourt, Brace & World for the lines from E. M. Forster, *Two Cheers for Democracy,* and to The Johns Hopkins Press for the lines from *Mallarmé: Selected Prose Poems, Essays, and Letters,* translated by Bradford Cook. 72146

Juan Ramón Jiménez

Strolling under the Puerto Rican sun, his ascetic figure gently bowed, the eyes dark glowing sentinels over a trim white beard, Juan Ramón Jiménez would often in the final years of his life shake his head and sadly remark that he had written too much, and that he would never live to edit the ceaseless flow from his pen. More than thirty books, with material for additional volumes, plus hundreds of aphorisms, constitute the labor of half a century on the part of this assiduously dedicated Spanish poet.

Juan Ramón, as he is universally known in the Hispanic world, was born in Moguer in Andalusia, December 23, 1881, into a well-to-do family that had made its money from wine. He attended a Jesuit academy in Cadiz from 1891 to 1896. A schoolboy copy of *The Imitation of Christ* by St. Thomas à Kempis foretells through such underlined passages as "Show not thy heart to every man," the strong adult penchant for solitude. He began the study of law at the University of Seville in 1896, but, since he preferred to paint or to read the French romantics far into the night, he soon withdrew. During his student days in Seville, he was primarily interested in painting, but he also wrote poetry and learned much of Bécquer by heart. More and more he turned to verse, and eventually some early poetry printed in provincial reviews attracted the attention of the leaders of the modernist movement in Spanish poetry, who in 1900 invited him to Madrid. Two books, redolent of modernism, were published almost at

[3]

once, and in later years vigorously disowned by their author.

One summer night in 1900, shortly after Juan Ramón had returned home to Moguer, his father died. The poet remembers the screams of women filling the house and his horrified conviction that he himself would also die immediately. He sank into a neurasthenic and incapacitating melancholy, in which state he was taken "half mad" to the sanitarium of Castel d'Andorte in Bordeaux. During the slow process of recovery, he began to write again, and for the next year occupied himself with the task of ridding his lyrics of the more pompous trappings of modernism.

Moody, petulant, and restlessly experimenting with different poetical forms, Juan Ramón was already an established poet when we met Zenobia Camprubí Aymar in 1912; after a long courtship, during which the pert young lady gracefully dealt with doubts about her somber suitor, they were married in New York in 1916. The influence upon Jiménez of this auspicious event can hardly be exaggerated. The voyage to New York brought him in contact with the sea, the most powerful symbol in his poetry; the North American background of Zenobia, who had been partly educated in the United States, introduced him to Blake, Shelley, and Emily Dickinson, an experience which caused him to qualify as "empty talk" much of the French and Spanish poetry he had heretofore cherished. Finally, the marriage gave him a common-sensical and cheerful partner, a foil for his often dolorous temperament, who, in the variegated role of lover, secretary, nurse, chauffeur, and mother, set about protecting her hypersensitive husband from the nagging details of life and fame.

Jiménez' poetry acquired a new sense of direction and his importance in the Spanish-speaking world grew rapidly. Back in Madrid, he wrote constantly, founded new reviews, encouraged young poets destined to greatness (Pedro Salinas, Rafael Alberti, Jorge Guillén), impatiently resisted fools, helped his wife translate Rabindranath Tagore, and acquired in the small intellectual circles of the Spanish capital a reputation for eccentricity. As the high priest of beauty in a cork-lined study, he was the butt of many a joke in Madrid cafés.

At the onslaught of the Spanish Civil War, Juan Ramón immediately aligned himself on the side of the Republicans, and with his wife took an active interest in a relief program for children, sponsored by the legitimate government. But the intense hatred now loose in the land made it impossible for Juan Ramón to write. He and his wife, having long planned a return visit to America where Zenobia had many relatives, decided to leave the Peninsula, engulfed in what the poet, with reference to the bitterness of Iberian character and history, called "the terrible Spanish war of three centuries."

In America, after a few days of trying to argue the Republican cause in Washington, the poet and his wife went to Puerto Rico and then to Cuba. In 1939 the University of Miami invited him to give a series of lectures, and thus began a long and fruitful relationship between Juan Ramón and American academic life. He taught and lectured at Duke, Vassar, and the University of Maryland. While in Riverdale, Maryland, he made the acquaintance of his favorite American, Henry A. Wallace. Jiménez was impressed that a man of such high idealism was also in a position of considerable prominence. "Are you really Vice President of the United States?" he recalls asking. "Yes, don Juan Ramón, I am," came the reply. "Why don't you take some of these tomatoes with you for lunch?" Finally the couple returned to the Caribbean, drawn by the climate that Columbus had said in his journal resembled Andalusia in April. He received the Nobel Prize for literature in 1956, the pleasure of which largely went unnoticed, because his wife died a few days later. Mortally stricken by this loss, he never wrote again, and died May 29, 1958.

As a good part of the civilized world heads swiftly into the arms of standardization, it may seem strange to insist on the importance of a regional influence upon a writer (although Ireland and our own South underline the effect of ingrained traditional cultures on literature). In any event, it is almost axiomatic that in considering a country like Spain, so late in reaping the unifying benefits of technology, the critic cannot slight the formative factor of *la patria chica* (the little country). Andalusia, with its unruffled blue sky and perfumed air, the clear profile of objects in its environment, its ready aesthetic response to the world, left a permanent stamp on Juan Ramón's mind. Formed in the mold of a Mediterranean landscape, this mind always sought synthesis in preference to discourse, harmony instead of logic. A Chilean critic even goes so far as to define Juan Ramón's strong streak of melancholy as the Mediterranean version of Kierkegaard's Nordic anguish. Be that as it may, at a time when Arab-haunted Andalusia had given to Spain two such poets as García Lorca and Antonio Machado, it was Juan Ramón who wore with ease the epithet *el andaluz universal* (the universal Andalusian).

Juan Ramón led a secluded life, and one misses at once in his poetry any sense of the "great world," or of the marketplace. For this reason, a group of young Spanish poets beginning to write after the civil war rejected him as being irrelevant to their time and place. These were the so-called social poets, who had discovered a willingness on the part of Franco censorship to permit symbolized discontent to appear in verse. In favor of the suffering and agony of the Spanish condition, these poets rebuffed the "aestheticism of the rose." They were stridently impatient with a writer who, interested exclusively in essences, could devote twenty years to transmitting all the nuances of feeling that grew out of watching a twig moving against the sky. Because of this over reaction, other critics felt it necessary to defend Juan Ramón's unrelenting pursuit of beauty. Meanwhile, as the quarrel simmered, Juan Ramon's international reputation steadily mounted. The entire argument has a paradoxical Hispanic flavor: on the one hand, Jiménez was the first poet to come out unequivocally for the Republicans; at the same time, the basic direction of his work remained serenely unaffected by the major catastrophe that had taken place in his country.

"Are you a *modernista?*" an admiring young lady of Moguer asked Juan Ramón in 1900, "and, if you are, what does it mean?" Juan Ramón was not sure, but he had read Rubén Darío, and, when sometime later he received a post card signed by Darío and Villaespesa inviting him to Madrid, he was filled, as he put it, with a mad, frenetic happiness.

Modernismo, in its broadest sense, is the Hispanic reaction in art and literature to the currents of change flowing through Europe at the turn of the century, currents best typified for the Iberian Peninsula by Baudelaire and the symbolists, but also Ibsen and Dostoyevsky, both of whom Galdós read and admired. In its more narrow sense, *modernismo* is the literary movement begun by the Nicaraguan poet Rubén Darío (1867–1916), who blended the rhetoric of Victor Hugo, the musicality of Verlaine, and the control of the Parnassians into verse that, in content and technique, was decidedly new in the Hispanic world. Darío's themes were limited—eighteenth-century Versailles, moody princesses, swans, and Nordic myths—but his poetic skill was superb, and his lines have an elegance and a sensual delight that stand in sharp contrast to the prevailing Spanish poetry at the turn of the century.

[7]

Juan Ramón's first two books, *Ninfeas* and *Almas de violeta*, are strongly marked by modernism. Printed in 1900, in green and violet ink, respectively, they proclaim the expectedly high-flown summons to the banner of art, and announce that beauty is the sole criterion of life. In their animosity toward prevailing taste and their desire for renovation, these books are part of the beneficent influence of modernism in Spain; unfortunately, they are in themselves generally tasteless, tending to be vulgarly sentimental and pointlessly prolific. They also possess a note peculiar to their author: a cloying morbidity encountered in connection with the death of a lover. In the thousands of flowers and tears rained down upon virgin cheeks resting against satiny coffin pillows, we may recognize two factors: the hypersensitivity characteristic of the early Jiménez style, and the already imposing fear of death that will, on occasion, choke his personality. Both problems must be overcome, or, at least, sublimated in his rise to greatness.

It was while recovering from his nervous illness in Bordeaux that he first managed to set his poetry in the direction he wanted it to take. With the wings of madness often brushing his face, he began work on *Rimas*, published in 1902. This is the first of his books to suggest a highly endowed poetic talent in the making. To Ricardo Gullón, he remarked that a nostalgia for Spain was behind the composition of *Rimas*, and this can be attested in the echoes of the *romances* (Spanish ballads), Andalusian popular songs, and especially, of the nineteenth-century Spanish poet Bécquer (1836–1870), whose poetry, too, was called *Rimas*.

Bécquer can be overly sentimental but never diffuse, sad but not complacently morbid, and these were qualities that Jiménez took to heart as he struggled in Bordeaux. Half a century later, the Nobel prize winner paid this simple tribute: "In Bécquer I discovered brevity and concision." He also felt

drawn to Bécquer's lesson that poetry should concern itself
with the ineffable, the light and airy, the perfect and therefore
unattainable love, and that the poet must constantly struggle
with the clumsiness of language which seemed to align itself
against pure expression.

In *Rimas*, Juan Ramón is still mourning the death of a
sweetheart, and he is still hopelessly sad: "I suffer forever a
snowfall within," but there is a sensitivity toward landscape
not formerly present and, above all, a simple, direct, clear, and
delicate tone that, in its rare appearances, gives us the first
inkling of the great talent to be developed. "El alegre mes de
mayo/ha nacido esta mañana. . . ." ("The happy month of
May/was born this morning. . . ."), These bell-like lines,
with their unobtrusive consonance and their gentle suggestion
of May songs, are an example of that *poesía desnuda* (unadorned poetry) that the mature poet will single-mindedly
court.

Instant critical acclaim greeted the publication of *Arias
tristes* in 1903, and today it is generally conceded that this
charming, sustained book is Jiménez' first noteworthy achieve-
ment. The work is a sweet, tuneful hymn to sadness, not the
affected and mawkish *tristesse* of the early poetry, but rather
a gently irrepressible melancholy that views every afternoon
as a quiet rehearsal for the close of life and assuages itself
with gentle sounds and a preference for penumbra.

In addition to the title, a framework of printed scores from
Schubert stresses the musical nature of the book. Jiménez had
read Verlaine in France and from the famous enjoinder about
the importance of music in poetry took to heart the idea of a
weightless song: "Sans rien en lui qui pèse ou qui pose." *Arias
tristes* is full of melodious, nostalgic music, very little weighted
by words (it is the sentiment which lies heaviest). But most
important of all, the book introduces a new note of simplicity

[9]

and delicacy in its diction. This is the tone and vocabulary that will gradually develop into the most winged and graceful verse in Spanish letters since the sixteenth century:

Entre el velo de la lluvia
que pone gris el paisaje,
pasan las vacas, volviendo
de la dulzura del valle.
Las tristes esquilas suenan
alejadas, y la tarde
va cayendo tristemente
sin estrellas ni cantares.
La campiña se ha quedado
fría y sola con sus árboles;
por las perdidas veredas
hoy no volverá ya nadie.
Voy a cerrar mi ventana
porque si pierdo en el valle
mi corazón, quizás quiera
morirse con el paisaje.

Between the veils of rain
that cover the fields with gray,
the cattle are coming back
from the sweetness of the valley.
Their sad bells ring
far off, and the afternoon
falls dolefully down
without a star or a song.
The countryside is grown
cold, alone with its trees;
by these lost pathways
none will return today.
I shall close my window,
for if my heart in the valley
wanders, perchance it will
die with the landscape.

When the poet moves from the countryside to an Andalusian patio, flowers become profuse and in the center of the scene is a fountain, its diamond-like thread pulsing skyward. Jiménez' early descriptions of a fountain suggest Georges

Rodenbach as a source, but he goes on to develop the fountain into one of his basic symbols, the ascension through lyrical expression to higher levels of awareness. Among flowers, Jiménez eventually chose the rose as a symbol of beauty and perfection, " a brief image of the world." When a poem is perfect, he later says in a celebrated verse, it is like a rose and should not be changed in any way. These objects are present in *Arias tristes*, but because they are overwhelmed by the languid sentimentality of the book, they do not yet function as efficient symbols.

The horror of death never abandoned Juan Ramón, but in *Arias tristes* he was able to sublimate it more effectively, at least as far as poetry was concerned. One night in his garden, he saw a man in black smiling at him through the shrubbery and drawing close. He fled to his room, only to find the man waiting for him, perched in a tree outside the window. The paraphrase of this well-known poem shows that in the image of the unknown man in black Jiménez created an authentic tingle of fear that was never elicited by his earlier scenes of lifeless virgins reposing in coffins. Also, in this book the author first asks a momentous question: what will the world be like without him? Common sense dictates the initial answer: the piano will continue playing even though he is not on hand to hear it. But, as we shall see, the mature poet tends to doubt, if not completely reject, the common-sense notion of his relation to the world.

A stay in the Guadarrama Mountains north of Madrid accounts for *Pastorales*, written in large part in 1903, but not published until 1911. In these poems, Jiménez continues what has been called his simple confrontation with the countryside, an encounter free of the sermonizing of Horace and far removed from the uproar produced whenever the romantics viewed nature. Segments of this work must have been closely

[11]

influenced by Francis Jammes' beatific nature poetry, which had made Yeats weep; and in Jammes at this time Jiménez may have read of "l'âne si doux," the gentle donkey, forebearer of Platero. *Jardines lejanos* (1904) is spiritually akin to *Arias tristes*, although more sorrowful. It is the last of the trilogy that gave new direction to poetry in Spain and prompted a letter from Antonio Machado: "A spirit as sensitive as yours does not exist among us; no one has such sweetness of rhythm, such delicacy for dampened harmonies."

Sick at heart from the hypochondria that he could not overcome, Juan Ramón returned to Moguer in 1905; he was, as he wrote to Unamuno shortly after arriving, "devoured by a yearning for contemplation." During six years in the village where he was born, he wrote poetry that, in a general sense, is a continuation of the work already begun, with no truly significant change. The favorite themes remain: love lost or unattainable, a sensual weariness, solitude, beauty; the favorite objects of nature still provide background: flowers, water (fountain), birds, and moonlight. With an indifferent munificence, he displayed a complete mastery of technique; no device was unyielding to his craftsmanship. Skillful enjambment causes the heretofore sturdily monotonous ballad meter to flow like water, and his alexandrines, whether with full rhyme or assonance, are as supple as his shorter lines. There is ample proof that from a technical point of view Jiménez could do anything he liked with Spanish verse (only the sonnet remained to be conquered a few years later). *Las hojas verdes* (1906) [dates refer to time of composition] is heavily touched by Verlaine. *Baladas de primavera* (1907) offers a collection of the light songs he could always do so well; added to later versions is the lovely poem of the greenfinch ("Verde verderol"), whose music in the dusky pine grove makes the wind stop and listen. Between 1907 and 1908 he wrote a series of elegies (*Ele-*

gías puras, Elegías intermedias, Elegías lamentables) which reveal a skillful use of synesthesia. *La soledad sonora* (1907), a title taken from St. John of the Cross, finds him still proclaiming in the symbolist manner that the essence of poetry was "an indefinite vagueness of forms and tones." *Poemas mágicos y dolientes* (1909) pleases by its use of color, and there are explicitly sexual memories of Francine, a servant girl he met in the Pyrenees. *Melancolía* (1910–1911) recalls his travels at the turn of the century, in particular a train trip through the Pyrenees, punctuated by "momentary villages." *Laberinto* (1910–1911), gracefully dedicated to seven women in his past, contains images that tend to be slightly more provocative and varied than those of the previous books.

The total performance is impressive in terms of technical variety and there are moments of genuine beauty, but the modern reader turns away, weary of such relentless, although strangely tepid, emotion, and it is at this point that one needs the corrective reminder of Professor Durán that Jiménez is more than a "sentimental, occasionally vulgar poet, read on Sunday afternoons by old maids who also own several cats and canaries."

The masterpiece of these years in Moguer has come down to us in the prose form of *Platero y yo*, although its evanescent vignettes are as lyrical as any poetry, and indeed show an attention to rhythm that is beyond the demands of even the most scrupulous prose ear. A common device, for example, is to place a descriptive adjective before and after a noun (*amplia verdura rendida*, broad exhausted greenness), thus bestowing upon countless lines a stately slowness. *Platero y yo* must be, after *Don Quixote*, the most widely read book in the Hispanic world. The little donkey with jet black eyes, gentle ways, and a brisk trot carries the poet into the corners of Moguer and over the Andalusian landscape. Together they

[13]

watch sunsets, ride through showers, gather wildflowers, and in general shun the company of their fellow men. While the entire village attends a bullfight, Platero and his master ride out of town, the shouts of the ring growing fainter as they approach the sea. In a note of pantheism that will grow stronger, Jiménez feels his spirit become ruler over nature, who, in payment for his regard, offers the eternal spectacle of her submissive beauty.

In its shimmering blend of colors and sounds, *Platero* is, in many respects, the culmination of Jiménez' impressionistic early years; with the shaggy donkey as a confident, the melancholy is better controlled, the sadness sweetly directed to a telling commentary on the world. Although man and donkey eschew large groups, there are, nevertheless, notable portraits of individuals: the kindly, toothless Doctor Darbón, whose laughter at the sight of children, flowers, or Platero always ends in wordless tears; Anilla, the butter maker, who every night dressed up as a ghost, and was finally struck by lightning and blackened forever; the idiot boy presiding silently in his doorway over the town's coming and going. These poignant notes from the severely circumscribed life of a village in an almost pastoral economy fulfill the subtitle "Andalusian Elegy" that the author appended to this extraordinarily gentle and wise book.

Enrique Díez-Canedo, reviewing *Baladas de primavera*, remarked that these songs were merely the variations of a preoccupied man who in reality wanted to write about something else. That topic was his own profound and engrossing sadness, which, as we have seen, he was rarely able to relegate to any minor role in his poetry. When he was sixty, Juan Ramón defined his sadness as "the anguish of the adolescent, the young man, and the mature person who feels himself unattached and alone in his vocation." This observation in middle age gives the overwhelming melancholy of his youth a certain dignity which one does not always detect in those early works written in Moguer. His sensitivity was unusual and his need for solitude acute, but the melancholia of those days, when it was not bordering on complacency, certainly threatened to stifle him and to curtail the range of his emotions. His future wife, in her youthful gayety, reacted at once to the cloud of gloom around her poet's brow. It was she whose teasing laughter caused his spirit to brighten in spite of itself, and enabled his mind, no longer clotted by sadness, to exercise greater control over the expression of his emotions. The letters of their courtship are marked by pertinent advice from Zenobia: "You need to break out of that woebegone rut." And on another occasion: "To my illustrious friend Juan R. Jiménez, in deep gratitude, for having seen him smile on August 10, 1913." He met Zenobia in 1912, and shortly afterwards a new note of assurance and a more searching quality appear in his verse.

The sonnet had been, except for one or two instances, carefully avoided by Jiménez until 1914 when he began a series that would total fifty-two and be published in 1917 as *Sonetos espirituales*. While adhering strictly to the classical rhyme scheme and to the convention that the theme is presented in the quartets and resolved in the tercets, he subtly experimented with the internal accents of the hendecasyllable, giving his sonnets a tenuousness that belies their strict form. These compositions do not suffer when compared to the classical models of Garcilaso or Fray Luis de León, and their existence is one of the reasons why the sonnet has enjoyed such popularity in recent Spanish poetry, as witness Rafael Alberti and Miguel Hernández.

The fortunes of his love for Zenobia form one of the themes of this book, and several sonnets protest, in a Patrarchian manner, the neglected feelings of the lover. More than once he tries to arm himself against her influence:

> Mas el dormir me ata con tus rosas,
> y tú te entras, cruel y desveladora,
> por la puerta vendida de mi sueño.

> But sleep binds me with your roses,
> and you come in, vigilant and cruel,
> through the door betrayed in dreams.

Most important of all in these sonnets is a new note of enhanced self-awareness that will become the characteristic mark of Jiménez. He began to realize that refinement of experience, simple everyday encounters with the objects of this world, could be the keynote of great poetry, and that for such refinement, the spirit, the poetic awareness, was a priceless alembic:

> Signo indeleble pones en las cosas.
> Luego, tornada gloria de las cumbres,
> revivirás en todo lo que sellas.
> Tu rosa será norma de las rosas,
> tu oír de la armonía, de las lumbres
> tu pensar, tu velar de las estrellas.

> On objects you inscribe indelible signs;
> then glorified by light from peaks,
> you live again in everything you mark.
> Your rose will be the norm of every rose,
> your ear of harmony, your mind a pattern
> for all flames, your vigil goal of every star.

Jiménez' next book *Estío*, written in 1915, is clearly concerned with the theme of love, not, however, in the Petrarchian manner, but more in terms of a spiritualized, ideal love presented symbolically. The pronoun *tú* refers on an obvious level to Zenobia, but it also stands for beauty, poetry, creativity, or the concept of love (at once palpable and abstract), so that the poet can say in striking assonance: "Pasan todas, verdes,

[16]

granas . . . / Tú estás allá arriba, blanca" ("Gaudy and green they all go by . . . / You are white and over all"). This love affair will now consume his destiny, and it will be love in the ecumenical terms of the world and I and beauty. Its union is unwitting and therefore perfect: you and I, he writes, are like the sea and sky, one without knowing it. And when he is guided to this love by a woman, a poem, a flower, a bird, he will feel the force and mystery of its immanence: "Eres ignorada,/ eres infinita,/ como el mundo y yo" ("You are unknown,/ you are infinite,/ like the world and I"). We have progressed a long way from the tired sensuality of the *Elegías* or *Laberinto* (books which rightly enough Zenobia disliked).

When Jiménez boarded ship at Cadiz in January 1916 to sail for New York, he was keeping a double rendezvous with destiny. The ship was to carry him to his future wife and also provide an intimate encounter with a great natural force. The record of this voyage was first called *Diario de un poeta recién casado*, but in 1948 was changed to *Diario de poeta y mar* The change of titles is significant, for although love plays an important part, it is the presence of the sea which dominates the book, even to the extent of influencing the meter. Jiménez later claimed his use of free verse in this book was due to the waves, to his not feeling "firm and secure." He thought the *Diario* his best book, and critics generally agree that it is the finest example of modern symbolism in Spanish poetry.

Jiménez found the very depths of his nature bestirred by this ocean voyage. Thrust upon him in all its force, literally clamoring for clarification, was the puzzle of the true nature of the relationship between man and the world as signified by this small dot of consciousness on the implacable sea. How to incorporate such vastness into a mind that had been attuned to sweet chords from Andalusian landscapes or had dwelt for hours on the perfection of the rose was a riddle in creativity, and in the end, he apprehended the image of his own mental process in the ocean's rapidly changing, yet fixed, nature.

The book begins in Madrid. Uprooted, in motion toward the port of embarkation, the poet is dwelling passionately on his love as the train wends its way to Moguer. At the scene of his childhood, he is overcome momentarily by the reality of the past suddenly become here and now. Yet all is falling toward the sea, which, while he is on the edge of it, is, in one of his favorite similes, as indescribable as woman.

He embarks, and the theme of love disappears almost at once, submerged for the time being in the depths of the imposing, gigantic body of water. Initially, the ocean appears to him as the personification of solitude, so dear to his way of being. Its waves come and go, like his fluctuating thoughts, in eternal knowing and unknowing. (Later on, his favorite line in "Le Cimitière Marin" was: "la mer, la mer toujours recommencée!") Everything is in the sea, and yet the sea seems to be without itself, lacking identification. The solitude has no inner warmth. Stupified, Jiménez begins to rebel at the limitations of language. The sensation of something so imperative, incomprehensible, and separate from himself creates one of his new preoccupations: nomenclature—the art of choosing the exact word. Neither the sea, nor the sky, as characterized by the sea, has a name. Until he can learn the proper designation, he cannot make the sea his own; baptism, or creation, is an act of identification and, thereby, possession. The early pages of the *Diario* make frequent recourse to the word *todo*, and that is the initial name of the sea: all, everything—strange, aloof, vast.

Accompanying the wonder before this event of wind and wave is the opposite reaction of distress and revulsion before the enormous mindlessness of the sea. One day, during his endless pondering upon the water, the word *nada* suddenly took on pefect meaning, finding its exact site, says Jiménez, like a body in its grave. Thereafter, *todo* and *nada* were used interchangeably, in a paradox similar to the mystics.

Arriving in New York, he recorded penetrating prose observations about life in the United States, overstuffed hotels and Brahman Boston, and wrote tender love poems to his bride. But when the couple embarked in June on the return voyage to Spain, the ocean once again became the chief protagonist. Now he can accept the sea; it stands before him naked, unadorned (*sin nada*), pure, as he will forever want his verse to be. And in an act of baptism, he proclaims simply, "Today sea, thy name is life."

On the return voyage, he gave the first unmistakably clear expression of a mystical desire to transcend himself, an impulse which, as we shall see, would gradually rule him. Gazing at the roadway the moon lays down upon the sea, he suddenly felt seized by a *gana celestial* ("celestial need") to leave himself and go to some undefined center. *Centro* becomes with *todo* and *nada* part of the new vocabulary that will stand alongside *rosa, mujer*, and *fuente*.

It was at this point in his life that Jiménez cast a critical eye on all that he had done before, and pronounced it as a *borrador silvestre* (an uncouth rough draft). He set about systematically trying to destroy all copies of *Ninfeas* and *Almas de violeta* he could get his hands on, and condemned nearly everything else to be rewritten. About correction he had definite ideas. Poems were not rewritten, they were "relived"; that is, given the passage of years, it was impossible to return to the original emotional state that inspired the poem. He would never let his lines alone, and he confided to his biographer Graciela Palau de Nemes, "A poem is not finished, it is abandoned." The task that confronted him now, upon returning to Madrid was the purification of that excess of sentimentality and vocabulary that veins his early books. He was ruthless, and one is reminded of Mallarmé's remark in a letter of 1867, "My work was created only by elimination. . . . Destruction was my Beatrice."

The reader who comes to Jiménez through the *Segunda antolojía poética* (1898–1918), published in 1922, will think that here is a poet who never made a mistake, and never struck a false note. This deservedly popular book is the result of Jiménez' rigid self-criticism, but it provides very little idea of any poetic development. Nevertheless, the vademecum for any Jiménez enthusiast would have to be one of the anthologies, preferably the third (*Tercera antolojía poética*, 1957), put together by Zenobia and Eugenio Florit.

Eternidades (1916–1917; published 1918) contains two poetic statements of utmost importance. One is the famous metaphorical account of the evolution of his poetry: how it appeared first in innocence, gradually donned colorful but specious clothing to the poet's intense dislike, then discarded superfluous raiment until it was once again cloaked in a tunic of innocence; finally it disrobed and stood naked before him. *Poesía desnuda* is the Spanish equivalent of the *poésie pure* of Valéry, who meant nothing more complicated than poetry stripped of unpoetic or prosaic elements. As Valéry pointed out, the rudiments of pure poetry exist in every poet, but the idea of pure poetry, applied to an entire poem, signifies only an ideal: pure poetry must be looked upon as "almost impossible to attain in a poem consisting of more than one line." Jiménez went even further and said that the best poem was the unwritten one. Simplicity and spontaneity, the twin criteria of his verse, were the result of a long and careful preparation, after which the poem would result from the effortless combination of the smallest number of elements. "Only the right word, the most direct and close, without effort, but apt."

This aphorism leads us into the second poem from *Eterni-dades*. It is cast in the imperative mood, and begins: "Intelligence, give me the exact name of things!" Instead of the vague sensorial images and the constantly shifting impressionism of the *modernistas*, the poet requests the clear straightforward title. The single noun "tree," and not a metaphor, is sufficient to designate the appropriate member of the vegetable kingdom. "Let my word," he continues, "become the thing itself, newly created by my spirit." Here is the role of the poet, who takes words in their direct sense and rearranges them so as to add a touch of newness. There are three radii of meaning in the exact name: the label supplied by intelligence, the title provided by the things themselves, and the name bequeathed by the poet. These are the spokes of connotation that spread out from the exact, that is, pure name.

By now Jiménez had developed a preemptory sense of his work in its entirety, and he began to refer to it as *la Obra*. Troubled by the magnitude of the task, the rarity of perfect phrases, and the pressure of time, he chose as a permanent epigraph these lines from Goethe: "Like the stars, / Without haste, / But without rest."

In *Arias tristes* Jiménez had posed the question as to the continued existence of the world after his death, and, as we have seen, he gave the logical reply that things would struggle on without him. In *Eternidades* he changed his answer radically:

> Sé bien que soy tronco
> del árbol de lo eterno.
> Sé bien que las estrellas
> con mi sangre alimento.
> Que son pájaros míos
> todos los claros sueños . . .
> Sé bien que cuando el hacha
> de la muerte me tale,
> se vendrá abajo el firmamento.

[21]

> Well I know I am the trunk
> of eternity's tree;
> well I know the stars
> feed on my blood;
> that every noble dream
> is a bird from my net . . .
> Well I know that when
> death's ax cleaves me,
> the sky will come crashing down.

This splendid assurance is part of an ill-defined pantheism that may be detected in his work about this time, but it also reflects the growing sweep and increasing sense of grandeur of his own consciousness, that divine awareness that will live again in every "exact name" it renders.

The plenitude and air of satisfaction that characterize *Piedra y cielo* (1917; published 1919) make it one of his most pleasing and unified works. Death, fear, and depression, usually expressed through the image of the black wind or the presence of *la nada*, seem temporarily banished. There is a gratified sense of poetic labor, of coming and going among the books of his library. He approaches his poetry with a permanent but controlled haste, and likens his creative urge to a colt in May, "free slave of his intelligence." Ineffability, the theme he took from Bécquer, is given its most striking utterance: beauty is like a butterfly, we chase it here and there, close our hands on it, only to be left with nothing but the "form of its flight." A section called "Nostaljia del mar" recalls the ocean voyage of three years before, and contains the lovely sailor's epitaph: search the skies for his tomb, his death rains from a star.

Toward the end of this book, an unusual desire becomes noticeable: the poet wants to be everywhere, to enjoy everything, to lose himself in his world. A tiny leaf glowing in the sun stands for his wish to be beside himself and to alter for a moment his private reality. To put it simply, contemplation of beauty is not enough; he must join it, flow into it, become one with it. These moments of epiphany represent for the critic Sánchez Barbudo, whose study of Jiménez is one of the most effective we have, an overwhelming need on the part of the poet to conquer death through a realization of eternity. According to this interpretation, the record of Jiménez' poetry since 1916 is the search for these interludes of fullness.

One may also see in them a nascent mysticism. This is the natural progress that could be expected, given the exalted role in which Jiménez cast poetic consciousness. That spirit which was to seal everything with an indelible sign and to become glorious among mountain peaks quite easily began to develop into the mighty sense of consciousness that pervades mysticism. Being, says the Hindu mystic Sri Aurobindo, is supreme consciousness. In all ages and in all climates, the first stage of the mystical experience is this heightened awareness; over this threshhold, one steps toward the unifying vision which sees all things as one and swallows up the identity of the individual. Jiménez was clearly headed in this direction; just how far he would go remained to be seen.

The pronounced necrophobia that acutely afflicted him throughout his life appeared in various guises in his poetry, but none so arresting as those in *Poesía* and *Belleza*, both published in 1923 and containing work written since 1917. Instead of the array of coffins and withered flowers, we have the image of death, as the great knowledge of shadow, the end of a beautiful book, a fruit plucked in season from its branch, or a dark subterranean summer.

But Jiménez was not satisfied with a series of pleasant images, for these books include a handful of poems that provide a taut and wholly engrossing dialectic between life and death. Poem 126 of *Poesía* may be paraphrased as follows: Cord, binding tightly my life to life, bind, as you must, without slackening, at once, my life with death; do not place emptiness and tedium between each knot; do not leave my life vacillating with death. Cord, life, death: taut until the end, taut from the beginning. This extended conceit clearly states that life and death run along the same thread and that to think of one is to evoke the other. Unawareness of this intimate dependency accounts for the tedious vacancy that sometimes appears in our lives. Rilke said that whoever celebrates death, at the same time magnifies life; Jiménez would agree and point out that praise of life is also praise of death. The sets of contrary pairs reinforce the image of a rope being pulled at both ends: life-death, beginning-end, strong-hesitant.

Here is a literal prose translation of a well-known composition, also from *Poesía:* "How can I fear you, death? Do you not labor here with me? Do I not touch you in my eyes; do you not tell me that you know nothing, are hollow, unconscious, and peaceful? Do you not enjoy everything with me: glory, solitude, love, unto the marrow of your bones? Do you not endure life for me, death, erectly? Do I not bring and take you in your blindness like a guide? Do you not repeat with your passive mouth what I wish you to say? Do you not support like a slave, the kindness with which I obligate you? What could you see or say, where could you go without me? Might not I, death, be your death, whom you, O death, should, indulge, and love?" With its serenity and profound irony, this poem attempts to vanquish fear of death by establishing a physical and affective identification that translates death into man's terms and casts it in the role established by John Donne as "slave to Fate, Chance, kings and desperate men." The vocabulary depicts humble human acts: the familiarity of laboring side by side, the ironic intimacy of serving as blind death's guide.

Finally, we have the poem "Cenit" from *Belleza:* "I shall not be I, death, until you join my life and thus make me complete; until my luminous half closes with my dark half and I become eternal equilibrium in the mind of the world; half of me radiant, half of me in oblivion. I shall not be I, death, until you, in your turn, will clothe my soul in your pale bones." The laconic title "Zenith" completes the irony of this cycle of poems, each one stressing the theme that life and death are inextricably bound together. The peculiar triumph of these poems is not the recognition that death is ubiquitous, a fact that was always painfully clear to Jiménez; rather, their accomplishment is the placement of death on an equal and friendly footing with life. Together the two bend over in the fields, while life teaches death what to say and guides it through eternity. However enervating Jimenéz' morbidity was in daily living, we must recognize that in literature he was finally able to overcome his pusillanimity, and to write about death in terms as courageous and noble as those to be read anywhere. The theme as such, along with its attendant images, will now gradually disappear from his work.

During these fruitful years in Madrid in the decades between the wars, while Juan Ramón's influence was at its peak, he and his wife enjoyed considerable success with their translations of the works of the Hindu writer Rabindranath Tagore (1861–1941). Their common interest in Tagore dates from 1913, and it was one of their earliest bonds. When they first met, Zenobia had begun to translate the English version of Tagore's *The Crescent Moon* into Spanish, Juan Ramón immediately offered to help, and they began exchanging paragraphs. The poet insisted that Zenobia receive all the credit, and her name appeared as the sole translator in the immensely popular editions that were published throughout the twenties and the thirties in the Spanish-speaking world. The instant success of *La luna nueva* in 1915 created a demand for the works of the Hindu polygraph that, after their marriage, the two labored steadily to fill.

Juan Ramón's role in this task of translation was, as near as can be determined through letters and accounts of friends, from the very beginning more than that of mere editor.

Zenobia's letters before their marriage reveal that she thought Juan Ramón should receive all the credit. "It's a shame that you should let my name appear; you're simply stealing from me something very lovely made by yourself, and I will tell everyone about it." Among the papers left by the couple to the University of Puerto Rico, are some notes in Juan Ramón's handwriting discussing the method employed in the Tagore translations. "My wife did a literal translation [from the English version]; then I would look at her translation and the original English and try to give it a new arrangement without altering literal meaning. After that, I forgot about the translation and looked at the work from my own point of view."

This comment, which came to light in 1960, explains why Tagore, in Spanish, sounds so very much like Juan Ramón Jiménez. In fact, it is difficult to know where the one begins and the other ends. Jiménez, recognizing a spiritual affinity and working from the literal renderings of his wife, poured his own poetic personality into Tagore. A phrase from the English version of *Gitanjali* which refers to a star and a planet becomes, in Spanish, "las estrellas infinitas," or "sadness" becomes "no sé qué tristeza." In both cases one hears the unmistakable accent of Juan Ramón Jiménez. The *Times Literary Supplement* remarked that, whereas the Indian poet was not notable for his language, Juan Ramón remained always the master of the beautifully cadenced line. Jiménez would have been strongly predisposed to Tagore due to the considerable oriental inheritance of Andalusia, and he would have recognized, as did Yeats, that Tagore sprang from a tradition where poetry and religion are the same thing, a concept which Jiménez nobly expressed in the devotion of his work and in his theories of poetry enunciated in his last years.

Juan Ramón first began to take an interest in the art of

translating around 1912 when he contributed some versions for an anthology of modern French poetry. These were followed by his translation of Rolland's *Life of Beethoven* in 1915. One of Jiménez' first efforts to bring English poetry over into Spanish took place with Shelley's "Mutability." It had attracted him in 1915 when he used it as the epigraph for *Estío*, the first book in the new vein, and the translation is of that date. Once again Jiménez' accent pervades the Spanish result, but such an intrusion on the part of a highly developed writer can probably not be helped. Jiménez once referred to translating as recreating, and in this he was not far afield from contemporary ideas which hold that, in order to translate poetry, one must write a new poem, and which have fostered "recreations" or "imitations" by Robert Lowell, Randall Jarrell, and many others.

The interest in English poetry was fostered by Zenobia's background and resources in the English language, and her husband continued in his pioneering efforts to transfer the genius of English lyrics into Spanish. He left several versions of Blake and a complete rendering of Synge's *Riders to the Sea*, done in collaboration with Zenobia. In America, he translated a few poems from Eliot, Yeats, and AE. The couple obviously enjoyed working at this art for on their first lonely New Year's Eve away from Spain in 1937, Juan Ramón notes that they fended off utter gloom by reading and translating together from the *Oxford Book of Modern Verse*, edited by Yeats.

Jiménez' intense preoccupation with the limitations and promises of language is, of course, evidenced by the large number of poems he wrote about poetry, the several remarks duly recorded by friends, and by the statements in his prologues and letters. These utterances portray a man to whom the manipulation of language in the expression of feeling was worthy of

[27]

the ardor and devotion that members of a religious order un-
questioningly invest in their worship. Such high-minded dedi-
cation to the art of using words inevitably overflowed the genre
of poetry. In fact, in his later life Jiménez began to believe that
the notion of genres was somewhat arbitrary, and that it confused the clear threads of voice which, pushing against the
limits set by prose or poetry, sought only to be supple and intense. To an audience in Buenos Aires, he remarked that a blind
man listening to reading could only distinguish poetry from
prose by a pattern of rhyme; otherwise, prose, just as much as
poetry, depended upon rhythm and careful selection of words,
although it could never be as intense or as compressed as the
latter. To illustrate his point he read the first sentence from *Don
Quixote*, which breaks up naturally into octosyllabic units. He
might have read with equal success passages from *Platero*, for
it possesses, as we have seen, a diaphanous musical prose that
belies whatever pattern of arrangement it takes before the eye,
and exists as an orchestration of sounds that, except for their
form on the printed page, could either be poetry or prose.

Jiménez' growing impatience with these traditional labels
did not mean that he placed poetry and prose on an equal footing, but merely that he thought the borderline between the
two was sometimes artificial, certainly in respect to stanzas
versus paragraphs. Poetry would always be winged, intense,
and mysterious, but prose was not, as a consequence, required
to be pedestrian, loose, and obvious. That he wrote a great deal
of prose from the beginning we can see in the material edited
and collected from the Jiménez papers by Francisco Garfias.
Primeras prosas (1962) contains several pointillist exercises
written from 1898 to 1913. These pieces are accompaniments
to his poetry; they possess the same romantic sadness, simple
love of nature, and unceasing sentimentality that mark the verse
of the period, and one cannot refrain from thinking that they

[28]

are the residual, however pleasing, of his remarkable prolificacy. *Por el cristal amarillo* (1961) offers a wider and more mature range of articles united around the theme of childhood, memories of the "sea blue house" in Moguer where he grew up, the adults who influenced him, and a few impressions of Seville and Granada garnered from his visits as a young man to these cities.

After *Platero*, Jiménez' greatest prose work, and indeed one of the most unusual books in twentieth-century Hispanic letters, is *Españoles de tres mundos* (*caricatura lírica*) (1914–1940), published in Buenos Aires in 1942. The first of these lyric portraits came out in 1924, and thereafter with increasing regularity readers of Hispanic journals were treated to their acerb yet tender style. The Spaniards of three worlds (Europe, America, and the "other world") number sixty-one, and range from close friends to famous acquaintances to dead authors whose work had inspired him. The form continued to hold his attention until the close of his life, and he had prepared several more of these penetrating caricatures which he hoped to include in an enlarged edition.

The subtitle "Lyric Caricatures" tells the intent: he proposed to distort and exaggerate, as happens in all caricature, certain features and attributes of a person, not necessarily for a satirical effect, but rather to recreate, with a loving touch, the essential personality of the subject. The adjective lyric assures us that these word paintings will not fall into the mordant savagery of Quevedo, who mercilessly deformed his subjects and left not an ounce of normal flesh on their bones. Quevedo, however, is an antecedent for these sketches, because in their intensity and involuted structure they easily unite two of the characteristics generally associated with the baroque style. In his prologue, Jiménez said, "I think (and so did Quevedo) that in caricature the baroque is at its best."

[29]

With amazing regularity, Jiménez usually manages to set the tone of his caricature in the opening sentence. The portrait of Unamuno begins: "Has Don Miguel come out of his mountain range?" Immediately one thinks of the geographic reference, the Gredos Mountains to the north of Madrid, and then the mind flies to the west, to Unamuno's stronghold, the University of Salamanca. But there is also the suggested comparison to an animal that roams the mountains and occasionally appears below in the plains, or to an isolated mountain dweller who descends periodically for supplies. Unamuno came to Madrid infrequently in order to launch his diatribes in person against the intellectuals of the capital, gathering "supplies" for his ego. But he hated Madrid, and like an eagle (a simile which Jiménez pursues at once in the next line) soon returned to his crag, high above humanity. The sketch on Ortega opens with this phrase: "Distance defines him well." At once the reader recalls the air of removal, of Olympian withdrawal usually associated with the great Spanish thinker who wended his way through a "labyrinth of laurels." Caricatures can never, however, wholly escape a note of satire, and Juan Ramón's perspicacious eye spared no one a few ungentle jabs, least of all fellow poets like Jorge Guillén and Pedro Salinas. He was also very conscious of regional or national background, and, when drawing his portraits of dead writers, he carefully wove the features associated with the land of their birth into a kind of nimbus inseparable from their greatness: Cuba in the case of José Martí, Galicia in that of the poetess Rosalía de Castro.

The quality of Jiménez' descriptions can perhaps be glimpsed in this translation of the first few lines from the caricature of Francisco Giner de los Ríos, the widely respected educator whose life and intellect inspired a generation of writers: "He came and went like a flame in the wind. He shot up, a whistling serpent, spread out and caught fire, a sparkling vine of hot coals. Like a lightning-maned lion he pounced; he channeled a stream of pure gold. Without visible union, he appeared every-where: thin, airy, unattainable in the absolute elasticity of a diabolical flame."

The reputation of Jiménez as a recluse is nourished by many anecdotes, none so typical as the one concerning Valéry's visit to Madrid in 1924. The great French poet was to lecture at the Residencia de Estudiantes, and Jiménez, certainly the most influential poet writing in the Spanish language at that time, recognized that the proximity of two such spirits deserved some recognition. However, he abhorred all public acts, especially those in connection with poetry, and never attended, nor gave, any readings. True to his dislike, he accordingly wrote Valéry: "Before a poet as secret, exact, and unusual as you, my greatest homage will be to forego the pleasure of your *persona;* words, phrases, gestures: what are they but the vicious rhetoric of the body?" In this apology, there is at least tacit recognition of the Latin etymon of *persona,* the mask worn by players, which came to signify the public covering that conceals the essence of the individual. Valéry responded with a poem dedicated to his distinguished Spanish colleague, the last line of which reveals that Valéry was content to savour from a distance the essence of Jiménez without knowing his person: "J'y respire un autre Poète."

Jiménez constantly refused to speak in public, but in the troubled summer of 1936 he was persuaded to lecture at the Residencia on the timely topic, "Política poética." How much this experience contributed to his transformation in America into "A sixty-year-old smiling public man" one cannot know. In any event, once on these young shores he broke out of his largely protective shell; he read the "Política poética" under the new title of "El trabajo gustoso" at the University of Puerto Rico in October 1936, offered a series of lectures in 1940 at the University of Miami, and carried his Andalusian accent in 1948 to Buenos Aires for talks before overflow crowds, which were enchanted to see the *persona* of the author of *Platero y yo*, whose essence had already engaged their attention.

His collected lectures were published in 1961 under the title *El trabajo gustoso*, and they are undeniably important as a commentary on his poetry and an example of his uncompromising idealism in life and art. "El trabajo gustoso" reads in some ways like an anachronism, and in 1936 in Spain it must have been greeted with cruel misunderstanding. Jiménez' basic thesis is that man naturally seeks a peaceful life and only deviates from it when his creative (or poetic) facilities are blocked. We are born, accommodate ourselves to our place, and, in so doing, experience the grace of existence, which is nothing more, nor less, than poetry. Man proceeds to build a house in nature, made with love, each addition carefully attached as needed. "That which is ordinarily called social war, civil war, race or class war, is nothing but the lack of design and love in the elaboration of our house; the lack of pleasure in the establishing of our life, singly and together." The happy society is the one in which we all work at what we like (Jiménez gives examples of a gardener, a mechanic, a coal dealer, and an irrigation worker, each one lovingly and creatively wrapped up in his labor); the origin of war is working at what we do not like.

The speech is remarkable for its refusal to come directly to grips with the political preoccupations common to the period, although the speaker is by no means ignorant of such themes. Instead, he prefers to abstract these topics and deal with them in his realm of pure poetry. For example, throughout the lecture he pays no heed to Marxism or dialectical materialism (concepts of extreme currency among intellectuals in the thirties) except to conclude, with no further nod toward the movement that was rocking the world, that man's natural state was one of lyrical communism, lyrical because it was beautiful and communism because it was common to all.

The basic beauty of life, Jiménez insists, begins with the act of birth, the opening of our senses for the first time upon the world. In this assertion, he is as far removed from the modern existentialist view of man's entrance into life as a purely gratuitous act as he is from that of his seventeenth-century compatriot Calderón, who in *La vida es sueño* had his hero take it for granted that "The greatest crime of man is having been born."

Despite its simplified idealism and its strangely abstract tone, "El trabajo gustoso" should not be too promptly dismissed. It is, for its time and place, an impressive record of optimism. The avowal that life should be sensitive, loving, and creative because it starts out that way in the initial communion between our senses and the world is basically a Garden of Eden myth, which no poet should be chided overmuch for cherishing. Furthermore, it is pertinent to remark that laboring at what we like (*el trabajo gustoso*) is no more fanciful on one level than the nineteenth-century doctrine of utilitarianism that proclaimed actions to be right in proportion to their usefulness or as they tended to promote happiness. John Stuart Mill's ultimate sanction was the "greatest happiness principle." Jiménez' was essentially similar: the happiness of the man who loved his work, whatever it might be, provided he was prepared for it and granted some freedom in selecting it. Jiménez does not explore these two vastly important qualifications, and he is, of course, talking about utopia. But those who overemphasize his neglect of society and the great world might read with profit this lecture and its companion, "Aristocracia y democracia" (1940), in which he defines aristocracy as a form of sensitivity and awareness for which democracy, far from being an end, is merely a preparatory stage. Jiménez would have had differences of opinion with E. M. Forster about art, but he would have been immensely pleased with this quote from *Two Cheers for Democracy:* "I believe in . . . an aristocracy of the sensitive, the considerate, and the plucky."

"Poesía y literatura," a lecture given at the University of Miami in 1940, provides a definition intended for a general audience of what he considered to be the qualities of great poetry, and it also offers a key to the verse he would write in America. He declares at the outset that he wishes to establish a distinction between "written poetry" and "literature." The adjective will come as no surprise to Jiménez' readers; it is his deference to the "daily weakness" that tempts a poet to try and set down in words the emanations of his feelings. Unfortunately, the only feelings worth writing about, according to Jiménez, are of such a remarkable degree of intensity that they cannot be properly recorded. "Written poetry" thus embodies a paradox, for it is the expression of the ineffable, the awesome, sacred feeling that defies utterance. All great poetry, states Jiménez with serene conviction, has its beginning in this emotion. Our courtship and cultivation of this feeling may take many forms (contemplation, mysticism, love), but the effort of expression always departs from visible reality and soars toward invisible reality. Poetry, he remarks in a most fortunate phrase, is a fusion of evidence and imagination. One of the exciting aspects of Jiménez' late poetry is his insistence upon the evidence of that most pressing and visible reality, the human body. The resultant tension between flesh and spirit informs many of his best poems written in America. As he said at the beginning of the *Diario*, one must have "roots that fly."

In order to express the ineffable, the poet must write in a state of ecstasy, or grace, from which flows his essential style. As Socrates tells Phaedrus, there is a possession and a madness inspired by the muses. To a certain extent, the poet is a medium, an outlet for the ascendant spirit. Possessed by a "possible god," he has no need for an absolute god, a concept invented by man in order to establish communication with the transcendental. Without reference to doctrine, in daily ecstasy, touched by grace, the poet soars on sacred wings, becomes for a moment the Platonic "soul" whose feathers have not yet fallen. "True poetry," Jiménez concludes, "is sustained by and rooted in reality; it desires by ascension to know invisible reality."

By contrast, literature, instead of being a state of grace, is merely a form of culture; it is concerned with relative and not absolute beauty; it is Plato's poetry of sense. In a later lecture, Jiménez employed a different nomenclature in order to make the same distinction: "open poetry" ascends, "closed poetry" tells a story.

In Spanish letters, the greatest poetry has been fatefully linked with mysticism, a statement which comes as no surprise since Jiménez insisted that the poet was a mystic *sin dios necesario* (without necessary recourse to a god). St. John of the Cross is the maximum example of great poetry: his talent, notable for its concentration in only seven poems, produced the purest lyricism in the language. Its fusion of inspiration, sound, and sense is breathtaking. Brevity, Jiménez says, is one of the basic qualities of true poetry, for ecstasy is always brief, occurring rapidly although seeming to last for some time, just as dreams appear to endure for hours when in reality they are over in minutes. Bécquer is, of course, another example of true poetry, as are Gil Vicente and the early Antonio Machado. Poets of *gracia intermedia* are Berceo, Lope de Vega, and Lorca; those who wrote only literature include Góngora, Quevedo, and Unamuno.

From this lecture we can extract the guidelines for the kind of poetry that Jiménez was to write for the rest of his life. The preoccupation with purity, the need to transcend, translate themselves into the spirit that seeks to dominate *La estación total* (1946) and finally breaks through in triumph to inform *Animal de fondo* (1949). It is a spirit enraptured, possessed by the gods of earth and air, a poetry of what Plato called "inspired madness."

[35]

The poems in *La estación total* were written between 1932 and 1936, and nearly half of them have as their subject moments of transcendant experience. Sánchez Barbudo's illuminating study takes great pains to distinguish between those poems which have the excitement of immediacy and those which are merely a nostalgic recreation of ecstasy, an intellectualization of a past emotion. Nearly all the lyrics in *La estación total* concerned with transcendental feelings fall into this second category. Although pleasingly gongoristic, and on occasion, of special beauty, they are not swept up in rapturous transport as are the lyrics of *Animal de fondo*.

"Su sitio fiel" begins with a description of landscape in which clouds, trees, and sun "fuse" into a single deep harmony; on the edge of this fusion, the sea, apparently in memory, rumbles and presses for admittance. There follows a recognition of what mystics call the undifferentiated unity of the world:

> El cerco universal se va apretando,
> y ya en toda la hora azul no hay más
> que la nube, que el árbol, que la ola,
> síntesis de la gloria cenital.
> El fin está en el centro. Y se ha sentado
> aquí, su sitio fiel, la eternidad.

> The rim of the universe slowly enfolds
> until everywhere in the blue hour
> there is only the cloud, the tree, the wave
> drawn together at the peak of splendor.
> The end is in the center. Eternity
> here, in its faithful site, is seated.

Whether or not one shares Sánchez Barbudo's opinion that this is a somewhat "cold" reconstruction of a past experience, one cannot deny that this stanza marshals many of the traditional elements of mysticism as found in practitioneers east and west. From the Upanishads to St. Paul to Arthur Koestler, one of the common characteristics of the mystical state of mind has been the unifying vision, the firm sense that objects lose their identity and flow together into what can be expressed abstractly by the formula "All is One." Thus, the Vishnupurana enjoins, "Let go the mirage of multiplicity." In Jiménez' poem, clouds, trees, and waves become cloud, tree, and wave, and are, in turn, drawn together in the synthesis of "la gloria cenital." In the unifying vision, it is usual for the ego of the beholder also to be dissolved, but in the poem under scrutiny, there is no direct reference to Jiménez' ego disappearing into Oneness.

The concept of the center has also always contained mystical connotations: to go within, to leave the circumference for the center is, in the words of Cirlot, to go from time to timelessness, from multiplicity to unity. The end of man is to discover the supreme purpose of the universe in its center.

There can be little doubt, then, that what had heretofore been moments of epiphany, radiant flashes of ecstasy permeated by a vague pantheism, has been converted into a concern which partakes of all the elements of formal mysticism. This transition began to occur gradually around 1930, and was coincidental with the general slackening of quantity in his writing and a return of his old despondency. *La estación total*, published in America in 1946, consists of poetry that was written in Spain, and, although he may have "relived" (his euphemism for "corrected") some of these poems in the United States before their publication, they nonetheless represent his state of mind from 1930 to 1936. The transplantation from Europe to America undoubtedly hastened the process that had begun in Spain, but it must be emphasized that the mysticism of his American period represents the logical development of his work. The prologue to the *Diario* mentions the oneness of feeling, and refers to his inner state as a "cluster of diversity" bound together in endless harmony.

One of the favorite symbols of myth, poetry, and folklore is the bird, long associated in nearly every culture with the soul. In Jiménez' heavily sentimental early period, birds and their songs provide sweet music in which the sad ego bathes, but in his purer style, he looked more and more to the bird as contributing to his transcendant spells, representing all that he desired to be: pure, self-sufficient song. The bird is truly, in his eyes, a "criatura afortunada," and in "El mirlo fiel," the blackbird, as did the graceful greenfinch long ago in *Baladas de primavera*, sings with such full-throated enchantment that its song transforms present reality, and turns the detained hour into eternity.

The final poem is in praise of the messenger of grace who bears the gift of plenitude. It was published in the influential Madrid newspaper *El Sol* one year before the outbreak of civil war, and its final stanza, set in the environment of imminent social chaos, quietly exults: "Messenger, you did exist. And I knew it."

The long prose poem "Espacio" provides another example of his basic indecision about genre. The first two fragments were published in free verse and bore the date, "Florida, 1941–1942." The next publication is not until 1954, the date of the third and final fragment, when all three parts appeared in prose, the form he finally chose for this particular work. Aside from an occasional comma, there is no significant difference between the version in free verse and that in prose. Jiménez probably selected the latter form because "Espacio," with its absence of rhyme, could not basically qualify as poetry. At any rate, the change confronts us once more with his preoccupation with form, and his desire to discover how the visual arrangement of words related to the total effect of poetry.

The dates of "Espacio" (1941, 1942, 1954) span almost the total period of his creative activity in America, and, therefore, the work as a whole is a valuable register of his growth during the last decade of his life. The first two fragments clearly reflect the confusion in his mind brought about by the ordeal of transplantation from one culture to another. Exile made him more than ever aware of man's odd relationship to physical reality—

the contingency of being in this time and that place. Hence the flow of adverbs in "Espacio," the constant qualification of a toponym with "here" or "there." Fragments one and two are a struggle to reassert his identity in a strange environment. The third fragment, written after the metaphysical éclat of *Animal de fondo*, shows a concern once more with death and the relationship between body and soul.

"Espacio" also merits attention because it is his first sustained attempt to write poetry in the New World. He informed the Spanish critic Díez-Canedo that "Espacio" was dictated by the smooth open terrain of southern Florida, whence undoubtedly the title. "It was," he continued, "a fusion in memory of ideas and anecdotes, without chronological order, like a film unreeled backwards in my life." Although it suggests automatic writing, as Sánchez Barbudo noted, the element of control is plainly present, and to a far stronger degree than that usually associated with surrealistic specimens of this nature. "Espacio" displays a succession of coherent unities, each one built around a single image or symbol. Since these are readily familiar to any reader who knows the Jiménez canon, the total experience of "Espacio" is like a loose, undulating review of his life and works. Although on occasion a scene is plainly labeled "here in Miami, Florida," the largest number of items in the poem have been released from the galleries of his memory to wander in free association in the present.

"The gods have no more substance than I," he begins in the first fragment, quoting a phrase he heard or wrote long ago. The assertion is unsurprising; on the one hand, the soul is itself godlike; on the other, Jiménez' efforts were always directed to elevating man's roots to the level of the temple. "I am a swordless god without anything men make from science, the product only of that which is alive." The man-god equation clearly foreshadows *Animal de fondo*.

If there can be said to be a link in the first fragment, it is the theme of love which runs like a golden thread through these loosely connected remembrances. Love, whether associated with the seat of excrement, as Yeats said, or placed alongside the life-giving warmth of the sun, is the single constant. "Love is one and only and returns each day." Love and light (or flame), which are traditional instruments of fusion in mystical testaments, play the same role in Jiménez, without, of course, any doctrinaire connotations. Another means of transcendant experience which makes its expected appearance is the bird: "You and I, bird, are one; sing to me, sing, for I hear you, my ear is perfect for your pitch." The first fragment finishes on a jubilant note that anticipates the unbroken optimism of *Animal de fondo:* "I with immensity. This is different; I never suspected it, and now I have it."

The second fragment is much shorter (only fifty-one lines), and begins with an evocation of the Hudson River that expands to include the sea in toto, and relates water to sun and love. New York's Morningside Heights and the Jiménez apartment in Madrid are the chief foci of memory, and there is a suggested confusion between the two points: "In the garden of St. John the Divine, the green poplars were of Madrid; I spoke Spanish to a cat and a dog; and the children of the choir, eternal language, were singing. . . ." Out of the confusion arises the simple but moving affirmation that time and space are "accidental frontiers," that the bearded, ascetic Spaniard is the same vessel of awareness whether buffeted by the wind in Madrid, wandering the streets of New York, or listening to a dog bark at midnight in Miami. The song alone is eternal and the language accessible to all.

The presence of a barking dog in all three fragments, as well as the foreseeable singing of birds, is clearly explained in the poet's own words. He kept a diary on the gloomy trip from Cherbourg to New York in 1936. The following passage was recorded shortly after his arrival: "Yesterday in Woodmere, the swallows by day, the dogs and crickets at night, drew me close to Spain, Moguer, Madrid, so joined together from this vantage point. It seems that animals (large and small) express in the same way their existence in every country. They alone have a self-sufficient means of universal expression. Later this evening Washington Square sounded, from a distance, with its cosmopolitan crowd like any Spanish plaza at dusk. Perhaps it's the same with crickets, dogs, and birds. Maybe the nuances of any language are lost in the distance. Perhaps, one day in the distance, all men will speak the same and understand each other."

The third fragment, begun in Florida and rewritten in Puerto Rico in 1954, well after the transcendental experience of *Animal de fondo*, is in many ways the most interesting of the segments of "Espacio." It is also the most confusing. In the first pages, Jiménez seems to be remembering in Puerto Rico things that he had summoned in free association from the past during the genesis of "Espacio" in Coral Gables, Florida. The line between the physical "here" of the body, and the mental "here" of memory is thoroughly confused. Nevertheless, the point remains clear that time and space are accidental boundaries, superseded by the ability of the mind to create a continual present. Thus did Juan Ramón react to the emotion of homesickness which is one of the chief motivations of "Espacio." There must have been a special poignancy in the fact that Coral Gables was so much like Andalusia (his letters are full of this similarity), setting up the fusion of present and past that characterizes "Espacio."

This final fragment shows a preoccupation with destiny. Before he died, Juan Ramón had planned to edit all of his vast writings under the single title of "Destiny." In the last portion of "Espacio," written after *Animal de fondo*, Destiny is capitalized, as the god of his sea mysticism never was, and is presented as a creative awareness of fate. Man should yield to destiny in the sense that a ship yields to the sea, not in order to capsize but in order to glide upon the water. The journey ends in death at the moment destiny determines, not before or after. "Destiny assumes many forms, death and life, taking and leaving; it is useless to flee it or seek it." It came to Shelley in the Bay of Lerici, to the criminal Barabbas freed in exchange for Christ; it was present in the instrument of the donkey that carried St. Paul to Damascus, and in the dray that killed Pierre Curie. Destiny, appearing as a final concept at the close of the heterogeneous work that covers all of its author's life in America, is an echo of the divine spirit that came to Juan Ramón on the last sea voyage of his life.

Animal de fondo, a hymn of triumph celebrating the highest level yet reached by his consciousness, was born during his third ocean voyage in 1948 to Buenos Aires. On the trip south he had felt himself once more aroused by the vastness of water and sky, and confided to his Argentine audience, "Life without the sea cannot be understood. All my experiences of eternity I owe to it; I have always renewed my poetry on the high seas." During the return voyage, he underwent what was clearly the most prolonged mystical experience he had yet known, as the "gana celestial," which had made its presence felt in 1916 on the Atlantic between New York and Cadiz, burst forth in twenty-nine poems, all of such sustained inspiration that one might believe the entire book to have been written in a single stroke. Significantly, he chose free verse to represent this enraptured state. Although some lines scan at seven or eleven syllables and there is even an occasional couplet, the general effect is one of fluid movement to which stanzas of poetry or paragraphs of prose are incidental boundaries.

A phrase from Carl Sandburg's *Poetry Reconsidered* has been tentatively suggested as the source of the title. It reads, "Poetry is the journal of a sea animal living on land, wanting to fly in the air." What probably attracted Jiménez to this statement, if indeed he had recourse to it, was the notion of man as a creature involved with three elements (water, earth, and air), yet not content to be identified permanently with any of them. He had climbed out of the sea onto the land, and now wished to continue his ascension. Nevertheless, although this idea reflects a view close to Jiménez' heart, a more likely source for the provocative title of his final book is the Platonic dialogue *Phaedrus*. Plato says that the soul when it is perfect and fully feathered roams the upper air, but once it has lost its feathers, it settles down to an earthly body and then takes on the name of "animal," which means a compound of soul and body. It is difficult to overlook this possible origin, especially since Jiménez remarked in 1953 that "Certain critics, who appear to be obtuse, might learn something from Plato." The closing poem of *Animal de fondo* has, it seems to me, strong Platonic connotations:

> . . . soy animal de fondo de aire
> con alas que no vuelan en el aire,
> que vuelan en la luz de la conciencia. . . .

> . . . I am an animal of the depth of air,
> with wings that do not fly in air,
> that fly in the light of awareness. . . .

Mortal man, locked on earth, yet possessor of a soaring consciousness, is coveted and inspired by a curious dynamic god, whose discovery constitutes the motive for celebration in *Animal de fondo*. In no uncertain terms, the first poem announces that this god is not a redeemer, brother, son, or father—in other words, not the Hebrew Christian God of Western religion. The god that appeared to Jiménez, as the bow of his ship plunged through the sea on the way to New

York was consciousness itself, the familiar divine awareness that had been called upon more than thirty years ago to place its indelible sign on all things. *Animal de fondo* is a paean to this god, who stands for the vast capabilities and transcendentalizing urge of the human mind. All former symbols, rose, love, woman, star, even the sea itself, were merely surrogates for this final divinity, the ultimate revelation to the devoted poet.

After being identified explicitly as consciousness (*la conciencia*), this god is given two permanent attributes that reveal its dynamic dual nature. It is a god desired and desiring (*dios deseado y deseante*). Desired by the poet as the ultimate level of existence, the *dios-conciencia*, by means of the active participle, also proclaims itself as desirous of the poet. But it is, at the same time, desirous of the world. The images of *Animal de fondo* show that consciousness seeks to expand, that awareness desires its own extension into the world in order to feed upon outside objects. Consciousness is within and without, desired and desiring, come from another star to the sacred well of the soul, and flowing back again in a constant giving and receiving. The *dios deseado y deseante* is an image of the poet's elated mind grappling with the world in a struggle of love that resembles the intense, rapid, yet tenuous relationship between flame and air.

One may be inclined to see the *dios-conciencia* as a mystical, somewhat more subjective presentation of Wordsworth's sublime spirit ". . . that impels/All thinking things, all objects of all thought,/And rolls through all things," with the reservation that Wordsworth's spirit would seem to originate from the outside and flow within, while Jiménez' takes the opposite course. Both poets emphasize the warm embrace between imagination and the world, and Wordsworth's classification of the mind and the universe as the one "insatiate" and the other "inexhaustible" comes close to Jiménez' view.

[44]

Animal de fondo is a mystical work, but with many qualifications. In traditional Christian mysticism, the body was considered an impediment and the senses had to be stilled, the devil of the flesh made to descend into the waters, as in the final image of St. John's *Canticle*, before the beatific vision could occur. Jiménez clearly explains in his first poem, "I have nothing to purge./All my impedimenta are but a foundation for this moment." He also exalts the body as part of the *dios deseado y deseante*, a sheath with a diamond in its center, and coins the word *cuerpialma* (bodysoul) to describe the intimacy between flesh and spirit. Therefore, despite the vocabulary common to the classical Spanish mystics (fire, flame, torch, love), Jiménez' book does not accord in a doctrinaire sense with this tradition.

Furthermore, we have seen that in the mystical state of mind, the one common experience is the so-called unifying vision in which all objects are synthesized into One. Examples of this multiply from *Estío* (1915) onward. But a corollary of the mystical unification is the merging of the individual consciousness into a universal consciousness, the single spark into the greater flame, until, in the words of Meister Eckhart, "The knower and the known are one." In *Animal de fondo*, this does not happen: the poet's consciousness flows out to the effulgent world and returns, ever more aware of itself and of the body which houses it. Jiménez' mysticism does not negate the individual: "Your glory in me and my glory in you," he tells his *dios*, who is "great and small in a proportion that is mine."

In the third fragment of "Espacio," given its final editing in 1954, we hear the poignant cry of a man only too aware of the reality of his body: "With great difficulty can flesh have loved its soul more than my body loved you (*conciencia*) . . . because you were for it the ideal sum, and it became through you, with you, what it is. . . . Tell me again: Do you not weep to leave me? Why must you leave me, spirit? Did you not like my life? I sought your essence. What substance can the gods give your essence that I could not give you? I have already told you: 'The gods had no more substance than I.' "

Like all great poets, Jiménez deeply affected the language of his time. For two decades, his style and tone dominated all other Spanish poets, with the possible exception of Lorca, making even the talented ones sound clumsy when compared to his pure lyric voice. After he jettisoned the excessive ornaments of his youthful verse, he was able to write a shimmering pure lyric that presented the most intense emotions in a deceptively simple way. His sensitivity permitted him to define ever more subtle nuances of experience. In the end, he discovered that the human mind, in the elation of poetic activity, was the most godlike thing he could ever know. Resisting all temptations, he espoused a secular religion in which poetry was the only rite, and its creation the only form of worship.

SELECTED BIBLIOGRAPHY

PRINCIPAL WORKS OF JUAN RAMÓN JIMÉNEZ

Poetry

Rimas. Madrid, Fernando Fe, 1902.

Arias tristes. Madrid, Fernando Fe, 1903.

Pastorales (1903–1905). Madrid, Renacimiento, 1905.

Estío (1915). Madrid, Calleja, 1916.

Sonetos espirituales (1914–1915). Madrid, Calleja, 1917.

Diario de un poeta recién casado (1916). Madrid, Calleja, 1917; title changed to Diario de poeta y mar. Buenos Aires, Losada, 1948; Madrid, Aguado, 1955.

Eternidades (1916–1917). Madrid, Calleja, 1918.
Piedra y cielo (1917–1918). Madrid, Fortanet, 1919.
Segunda antolojía poética (1898–1918). Madrid, Impr. Clásica Española, 1920; Madrid, Espasa-Calpe, 1955.
Belleza (en verso) (1917–1923). Madrid, J. R. Jiménez y Z. C. de Jiménez, 1923.
Poesía (en verso) (1917–1923). Madrid, J. R. Jiménez y Z. C. de Jiménez, 1923; Buenos Aires, Losada, 1946.
"La estación total" con las "Canciones de la neuva luz." Buenos Aires, Losada, 1946.
Animal de fondo. Buenos Aires, Pleamar, 1949.
Tercera antolojía poética (1898–1953). Madrid, Biblioteca Nueva, 1957.
Primeros libros de poesía. Madrid, Aguilar, 1959. (Ninfeas to Melancolía.)
Libros de poesía. Madrid, Aguilar, 1959. (Sonetos espirituales to Animal de fondo.)
Prose
Platero y yo, elegía andaluza. Madrid, La Lectura, 1914.
Españoles de tres mundos: Viejo mundo. Nuevo mundo. Otro mundo (Caricatura lírica) (1914–1940). Buenos Aires, Losada, 1944; Madrid, Aguado, 1960.
Monumento de amor. San Juan, P.R., La Torre, 1959. (Correspondance between Juan Ramón and Zenobia.)
El trabajo gustoso. Mexico, Aguilar, 1961.
Por el cristal amarillo. Madrid, Aguilar, 1961.
La corriente infinita. Madrid, Aguilar, 1961. (Criticism and personal evocations.)
Primeras prosas. Madrid, Aguilar, 1962.

Translations of Jiménez' Works

Fifty Spanish Poems, trans. J. B. Trend. New York, Oxford, 1950; Berkeley, 1951.
Platero and I, trans. Eloïse Roach. Austin, U. of Texas Press, 1957.
The Selected Writings of Juan Ramón Jiménez, trans. H. R. Hays. New York, Farrar, Straus, and Cudahy, 1957.
Three Hundred Poems, 1903–1953, trans. Eloïse Roach. Austin, U. of Texas Press, 1962.

CRITICAL WORKS AND COMMENTARY

Díaz Plaja, Guillermo. Juan Ramón Jiménez en su poesía. Madrid, Aguilar, 1958.

Díez-Canedo, Enrique. Juan Ramón Jiménez en su obra. Mexico, El Colegio de México, 1944.

Fogelquist, Donald F. "Juan Ramón Jiménez: Vida y obra," *Revista Hispánica Moderna*, XXIV (1958), nos. 2–3, pp. 105–77.

Garfias, Francisco. Juan Ramón Jiménez. Madrid, Taurus, 1958.

Givocate, Bernardo. La poesía de Juan Ramón Jiménez. San Juan, P.R., Asomante, 1959.

Guerrero Ruiz, Juan. Juan Ramón de viva voz. Madrid, Insula, 1961.

Gullón, Ricardo. Conversaciones con Juan Ramón Jiménez. Madrid, Taurus, 1958.

——Estudios sobre Juan Ramón Jiménez. Buenos Aires, Losada, 1960.

Neddermann, Emmy. Die symbolistischen Stilelemente im Werke von Juan Ramón Jiménez. Hamburg, Seminar für Romanische Sprachen und Kultur, 1935.

Olson, Paul R. "Structure and Symbol in a Poem of Juan Ramón Jiménez," *Modern Language Notes*, LXXVI (1963), 636–47.

Pablos, Basilio de. El tiempo en la poesía de Juan Ramón Jiménez. Madrid, Gredos, 1965.

Palau de Nemes, Graciela. Vida y obra de Juan Ramón Jiménez. Madrid, Gredos, 1957.

Predmore, Michael P. La obra en prosa de Juan Ramón Jiménez. Madrid, Gredos, 1966.

Romeralo, Antonio J. "Juan Ramón Jiménez en su fondo de aire," *Revista Hispánica Moderna*, XXVII (1961), 299–319.

Sánchez Barbudo, Antonio. La segunda época de Juan Ramón Jiménez. Madrid, Gredos, 1962.

Sobejano, Gonzalo. "Juan Ramón Jiménez a través de la crítica," *Romanistisches Jahrbuch*, VIII (1957), 341–66; IX (1958), 299–317.

Young, Howard T. The Victorious Expression: A Study of Four Contemporary Spanish Poets. Madison, U. of Wisconsin Press, 1964. [Jiménez, pp. 75–135.]

Zardoya, Concha. Poesía española contemporánea. Madrid, Guadarrama, 1961. ["El dios deseado y deseante de Juan Ramón Jiménez," pp. 217–40.]

Poetry, 82 (July 1953). [Issue dedicated to Jiménez.]

Revista Hispánica Moderna, XXIV (1958), nos. 2–3. [Issue dedicated to Jiménez, with bibliography.]

La Torre, V (1957), nos. 19–20. [Issue dedicated to Jiménez.]